DATE DUE

Grassland Animals

Coyotes

by Patricia J. Murphy

Consulting Editor: Gail Saunders-Smith, Ph.D.
Consultant: Marsha A. Sovada, Ph.D., Research Wildlife Biologist
Northern Prairie Wildlife Research Center, U.S. Geological Survey
Jamestown, North Dakota

Capstone
press
Mankato, Minnesota

Pebble Books are published by Capstone Press
151 Good Counsel Drive, P.O. Box 669, Mankato, Minnesota 56002
www.capstonepress.com

1 2 3 4 5 6 09 08 07 06 05 04

Library of Congress Cataloging-in-Publication Data
Murphy, Patricia J., 1963–
    Coyotes / by Patricia J. Murphy.
    p. cm.—(Grassland animals)
    Summary: Simple text and photographs introduce coyotes and their grasslands
habitat.
    Includes bibliographical references (p. 23) and index.
    ISBN 0-7368-2072-8 (hardcover)
    1. Coyote—Juvenile literature. [1. Coyote. 2. Grasslands.] I. Title. II. Series.
QL737.C22M79 2004
599.77′25—dc22   2003013417

Note to Parents and Teachers

The Grassland Animals series supports national science standards
related to life science. This book describes and illustrates coyotes.
The photographs support early readers in understanding the text.
The repetition of words and phrases helps early readers learn new
words. This book also introduces early readers to subject-specific
vocabulary words, which are defined in the Glossary. Early readers
may need assistance to read some words and to use the Table of
Contents, Glossary, Read More, Internet Sites, and Index/Word List
sections of the book.

Table of Contents

Coyotes

Coyotes are mammals in the dog family. Coyotes have strong jaws and sharp teeth.

Coyotes have gray, brown, red, or black fur. The tips of their tails are black.

Coyotes have pointed ears
and long, thin legs.
Coyotes run fast.

areas where coyotes live

10

Where Coyotes Live

Coyotes roam grasslands in North America and Central America. Grasslands are large open areas of grass.

Coyote Packs

Coyotes often live together in packs. Coyotes hunt in packs or alone.

Coyotes hunt small animals and insects. Coyotes also eat fruit and seeds.

Coyotes raise their pups in underground dens. About five pups are in a litter.

Coyotes are noisy. They yip, howl, and bark at other coyotes.

Coyotes at Night

Coyotes sometimes howl at night. Coyotes sleep outside under the stars.

Glossary

den—a home of a wild animal; coyotes often make their dens in other animals' burrows.

grassland—a large open area of grass; coyotes live on grasslands and near forests.

howl—to cry out loudly

litter—a group of animals born at the same time to the same mother

mammal—a warm-blooded animal that has a backbone; mammals have fur or hair; female mammals feed milk to their young.

pack—a group of the same kind of animals

pup—a young coyote; as few as one and as many as 20 pups may be in a litter; most litters have five pups.

roam—to travel across a large area

Read More

Barrett, Jalma. *Coyote.* Wild Canines! Woodbridge, Conn.: Blackbirch Press, 2000.

Gentle, Victor, and Janet Perry. *Coyotes.* Wild Dogs. Milwaukee: Gareth Stevens, 2002.

Whitehouse, Patricia. *Coyotes.* What's Awake. Chicago: Heinemann Library, 2003.

Internet Sites

FactHound offers a safe, fun way to find Internet sites related to this book. All of the sites on FactHound have been researched by our staff.

Here's how:

1. Visit *www.facthound.com*
2. Type in this special code **0736820728** for age-appropriate sites. Or enter a search word related to this book for a more general search.
3. Click on the **Fetch It** button.

FactHound will fetch the best sites for you!

23

Index/Word List

Word Count: 116
Early-Intervention Level: 13

Editorial Credits
Martha E. H. Rustad, editor; Patrick Dentinger, designer; Scott Thoms,
    photo researcher; Karen Risch, product planning editor

Photo Credits
Comstock Klips, 10
Corbis/W. Perry Conway, 4, 6
Corel, cover, 20
Erwin and Peggy Bauer, 1, 12, 14, 16
Minden Pictures/Konrad Wothe, 8
Richard P. Smith, 18